An opinionated guide to

OXFORD

Written by
HESTER UNDERHILL

Hertford Bridge

INFORMATION IS DEAD. LONG LIVE OPINION.

When we conceived these guidebooks, we feared they would fail. Who needs a guidebook when everything can be found online for free?

But then it occurred to us: that's exactly why you *do* want a guidebook. You want lively, trustworthy opinion, from a human being, combined with great photographs. You don't want endless information from a thousand online bots.

We think you are like us: you care about quality, you care about style, you care about provenance, but you don't have time to waste on long words like 'provenance'. You want to cut to the chase: where's good?

We are an independent from London. How dare we write a book about Oxford? Because we work with passionate local writers who seek out the spots that remind us of the east London we know and love: these are the most creative, diverse and exciting places of all.

Ann & Martin, co-founders
Hoxton Mini Press

JERICHO CHEESE COMPANY
Wild Honey
JERICHO CHEESE COMPANY
XPH 472Y

Estelle Manor (no.61)

Opposite: Jericho Cheese Company (no.30)

View from Old Bank Hotel (no.60)

Objects of Use (no.29)

Opposite: King's Arms (no.2)

THE KINGS ARMS
KING'S ARMS
TRADITIONAL PUB
YOUNG'S
AWARD WINNING
ALES
BRITISH
PUB DINING
HOLYWELL STREET

BEYOND THE DREAMING SPIRES

A phrase you'll often hear in Oxford is 'town and gown' – a term used to describe the divide between the university and the rest of the city.

The charms of the 'gown' side are easy to see: the ancient colleges, historic libraries, grand concert halls and cobbled alleyways filled with students rushing between lectures. This is the Oxford of popular imagination, the version of the city immortalised in everything from *Brideshead Revisited* to *Inspector Morse*.

It's this magisterial vision of Oxford that draws millions of visitors each year. Yet, as in many other classically beautiful European cities, these historic buildings are neither frozen in time nor merely ornamental; they continue to serve their original purpose as part of the university. Oxford therefore remains a living, breathing city – not simply a place preserved for tourists.

This prestigious 'gown' side is the focus in countless other guidebooks. In these pages, however, you'll find far more than the main sights, venturing outside the city centre to uncover the 'town' side of Oxford: the cosy neighbourhood pubs, riverside restaurants, independent bookshops and bakeries that make local life so appealing.

The quality and quantity of these businesses mean Oxford is becoming something it never was: cool. It's been quietly shaking off its studious and stuffy reputation; today, those in search of artisanal sourdough pastries, Japanese denim and small-plate dining no longer lack choice here. Recent years have seen east Oxford's Magdalen Road emerge as a particular culinary hot spot, while Walton Street in Jericho (a pretty residential quarter just north of the centre) has long boasted some of the city's most characterful bars and restaurants.

Metropolitan buzz aside, what really makes Oxford the perfect getaway is its abundance of bucolic greenery. This is a city where urban life spills seamlessly into water meadows, riverside paths and ancient woodland. Within minutes of the centre, you can find yourself punting beneath willow trees on the River Cherwell, strolling down shady paths in the gardens of Magdalen College (no.49) or watching cattle graze on Port Meadow (no.53).

This is a city that rewards wandering, and thanks to its diminutive size, you can really cram it all in. Just be sure not to rush your way through and leave plenty of time to admire the 'dreaming spires' – a phrase coined by Victorian poet Matthew Arnold to describe the city's skyline, which is arguably the most beautiful in the UK. Sorry, Cambridge.

Hester Underhill
Oxford, 2026

BEST FOR...

Rainy days

Shelter from the drizzle in the Ashmolean (no.42), Britain's first public museum, and get lost among its treasures. Otherwise, head to Christ Church (no.47), New College (no.48) or Magdalen College (no.49) to admire some of the university's most spectacular architecture from beneath the refuge of medieval cloisters and vaulted halls.

With kids

The Pitt Rivers Museum (no.40) is one of the city's great wonders, and its crowded cabinets of curios are perfect for sparking young imaginations. In the adjoining building, the Museum of Natural History (no.44) offers dinosaur skeletons and hands-on exhibits, while the expansive lawns of nearby University Parks (no.54) are ideal for picnicking.

Indie shopping

Clustered in and around The Covered Market (no.33) are some of Oxford's finest independent shops. Inside, check out stylish menswear store Goodies (no.35) and indie bookshop Gulp Fiction (no.32). On the adjoining streets you'll also find minimalist homeware shop Objects of Use (no.29) and characterful stationer's Scriptum (no.28).

Hearty breakfasts

Start the day right at Brown's Cafe (no.24), a local institution that has been fuelling students and locals with mighty fry-ups for generations. Over in east Oxford, Green Routes (no.8) specialises in excellent coffee and towering stacks of fluffy pancakes.

Sunday roasts

The Magdalen Arms (no.4) serves a mean Sunday lunch. Highlights include the pork belly with sage and onion stuffing, served with irresistibly crisp roasties. Alternatively, The Chester Arms (no.25) has been serving its famous steak platter since 2009, complete with homemade chips and lashings of béarnaise sauce.

Literary Oxford

Few cities can rival Oxford's literary pedigree. Raise a pint at the Lamb & Flag (no.18), once the watering hole of Tolkien and C. S. Lewis, browse the seemingly endless shelves of Blackwell's (no.34) or admire the grandeur of the Bodleian Library (no.39), one of the oldest libraries in Europe.

Sunny spells

When the sun appears, Oxford spills outdoors. Hire a punt at Magdalen Bridge (no.50) and go for a glide along the Cherwell or stroll along the shady paths of the Botanic Garden (no.52). And if you really need to cool off, make a beeline to Hinskey Outdoor Pool (no.57) for a restorative dip.

A PERFECT WEEKEND

Friday night

Make the chic Old Parsonage Hotel (no.59) – set within a wisteria-clad 17th-century building – your bolthole for the weekend. A short walk away, Gees (no.1) serves British fare within an elegantly restored Victorian glasshouse.

Saturday morning

Head to The Covered Market (no.33) for a robust fry-up at Brown's Cafe (no.24) or a pastry at artisan bakery Hamblin Bread (no.12). The market is strolling distance from all the city's main sights, including the Bodleian Library (no.39), Radcliffe Camera and Sheldonian Theatre.

Saturday lunch

For authentic Japanese home cooking, stop at Edamamé (no.15), a tiny eatery tucked away on pretty Holywell Street. And if it's a classic pub lunch you're after, the King's Arms (no.2) is hard to beat.

Saturday afternoon

A visit to Oxford's colleges affords a fascinating glimpse into university life. Magdalen College (no.49) is particularly charming; after admiring its elaborately decorated chapel, you can meander along the river through the college's picturesque meadow.

Saturday evening

Indulge in a French feast at family-run bistro Pierre Victoire (no.3), starting with the Maldon oysters followed by a generous serving of steak frites. If you're not too stuffed to move, The Bear Inn (no.21) – Oxford's smallest pub – is a cosy spot for a nightcap.

Sunday morning

Ease into the day with a coffee from Barefoot (no.17) before making your way to the Oxford Botanic Garden (no.52). Spend the rest of the morning wandering its leafy pathways, lined with all manner of peculiar plants.

Sunday lunch

For a proper slap-up roast, it doesn't get much better than The Magdalen Arms (no.4). Its delicious duck-fat roasties – served alongside succulent slow-roast pork or beef rump – are a particular crowd-pleaser.

Sunday afternoon

Try your hand at the ultimate Oxford pastime: punting. Pick up a boat at Magdalen Bridge (no.50) and drift along the willow-lined Cherwell. It's trickier than it looks, so don't be embarrassed to hire a 'chauffeur' if necessary.

Sunday evening

Round off your weekend at tapas restaurant Arbequina (no.6). Nab a bar seat to watch dishes such as chicken *al ajillo* and tempura courgette being whipped up in the open kitchen. Afterwards, catch a classic flick at The Ultimate Picture Palace (no.41), a historic gem of a cinema.

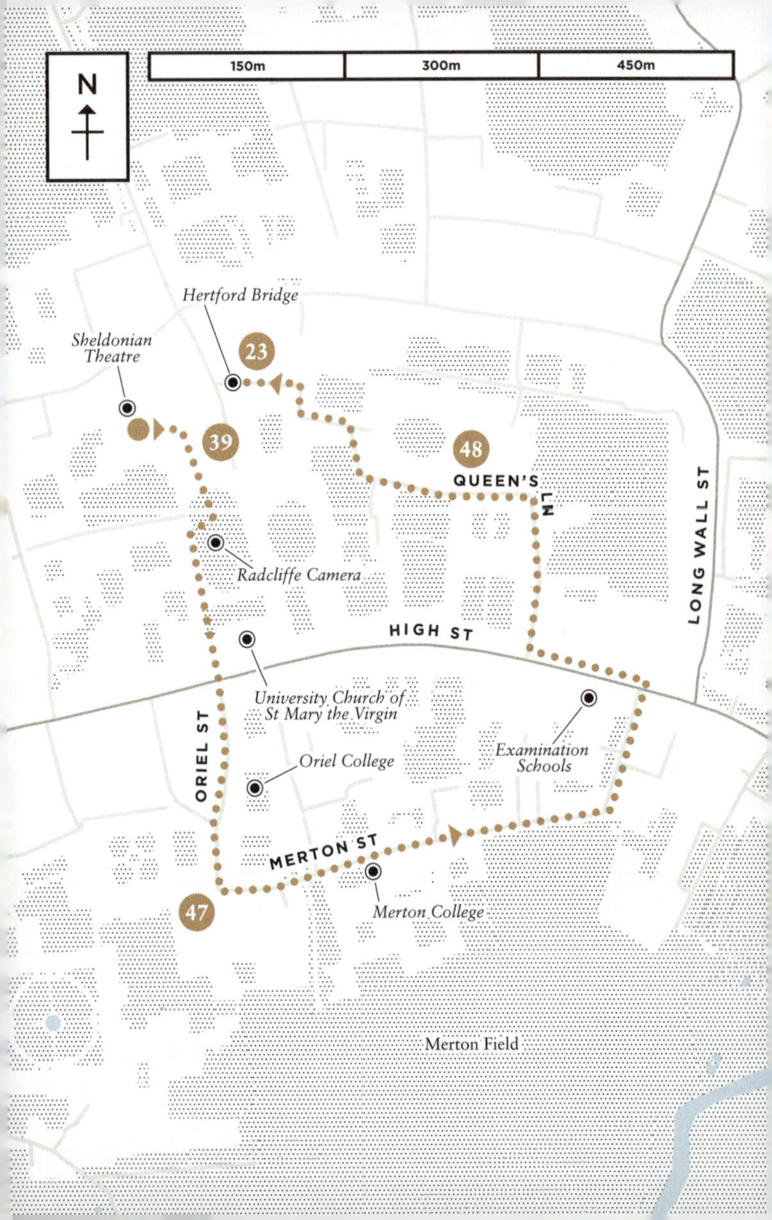
N
150m
300m
450m
Hertford Bridge
Sheldonian Theatre
23
39
48
QUEEN'S LN
LONG WALL ST
Radcliffe Camera
HIGH ST
University Church of St Mary the Virgin
ORIEL ST
Oriel College
Examination Schools
MERTON ST
Merton College
47
Merton Field

WALK A:
THE CENTRE

A compact tour of Oxford's magisterial architecture

Begin outside the curving walls of the *Sheldonian Theatre*, designed by Sir Christopher Wren in the 1660s. Then duck through the Bodleian Library's ❸❾ Old Schools Quadrangle and emerge into Radcliffe Square, its skyline dominated by the grand circular dome of the *Radcliffe Camera*. Continue down St Mary's Passage past the dramatic Gothic spire of the *University Church of St Mary the Virgin*, before crossing the historic High Street into Oriel Street. Follow the lane past *Oriel College* (taking a peek through the gates to see statues of Edward II and Charles I) and the rear of Christ Church ❹❼ to reach cobbled Merton Street, one of Oxford's most atmospheric thoroughfares. Pass the elaborately carved facade of *Merton College*, then continue to the end of the street and turn left past the Victorian *Examination Schools*. Cross the High Street and slip up Queen's Lane, a narrow street that snakes past the medieval walls of New College ❹❽. Finally, cut down the alley leading to the Turf Tavern ❷❸ and emerge next to *Hertford Bridge* – opened in 1914 to connect the two sides of Hertford College and frequently compared with Venice's famous Bridge of Sighs.

Length: 1.4km

Walking time without stops: 20 minutes

Start: Sheldonian Theatre

N
200m
400m
600m
BANBURY RD
KINGSTON RD
WALTON WELL RD
53
WOODSTOCK RD
20
JUXON ST
Blavatnik
School of Government
WALTON ST
55
9
LITTLE
CLARDENDON ST
Oxford
University Press
Castle Mill Stream
River Thames
ST GILES'
BEAUMONT ST
Oxford

WALK B: JERICHO

A canalside jaunt through Oxford's coolest neighbourhood

Start on Little Clarendon Street, stopping at George & Davis **9** to pick up a cone of lemon meringue ice cream. Take a right onto Walton Street to stroll past the *Blavatnik School of Government*, designed by architects Herzog & de Meuron. It drew comparisons to a huge glass spaceship when the building officially opened in 2016 and contrasts sharply with the grand neoclassical facade of the *Oxford University Press* headquarters opposite. Continue past the parade of shops, cafes and pubs – dropping in to cafe-cum-deli Branca **20** to refuel, if necessary – before turning onto *Juxon Street*, lined with neat rows of pastel-painted Victorian terraces. At the bottom of the street, hop over the bridge that takes you to the canal **55** footpath. Follow it to the right, passing colourfully decorated canal boats, until you hit the next bridge. From there, head along Walton Well Road to reach Port Meadow **53**, a vast expanse of open grassland that's a popular picnic spot on sunny days.

Length: 1.6km

Walking time without stops: 20 minutes

Start: Little Clarendon Street

N
200m
400m
600m
Park Town
DRAGON LN
FYFIELD RD
The Rose & Crown
Lady Margaret Hall
17
N. PARADE AVE
BANBURY RD
WOODSTOCK RD
PARKS RD
54
University Parks

WALK C: NORTH OXFORD

Escape the bustling city centre for leafier surroundings

North Oxford is great for exploring the city's prettiest residential streets and the smart independent businesses serving its well-heeled residents. Start in University Parks (54) and leave by the northern exit, following a narrow alleyway that takes you past *Lady Margaret Hall*. Continue north past the grand Victorian villas of *Fyfield Road*, then nip down Dragon Lane. Midway along, turn left to walk through a grand stone arch into *Park Town*. This elegant pocket of Regency-inspired stone crescents was one of the city's earliest planned suburbs, built in the 1850s. Stroll past its verdant gardens to reach Banbury Road, then cut west along *North Parade Avenue* – a pedestrianised side street home to many of the city's most characterful small businesses, from knitting shops and delis to pint-sized pubs. Wet your whistle at *The Rose & Crown* (its bright pink facade is hard to miss) or end your walk with a silky flat white and a slice of chocolate fudge cake at Barefoot (17).

Length: 1.2km

Walking time without stops: 15 minutes

Start: University Parks

1

GEES

Charming conservatory serving modern British fare

Gees is Oxford's prettiest restaurant, hands down. A ten-minute walk from central Oxford will bring you to this Grade II-listed Victorian glasshouse, built in 1897 to house the Gee family's greengrocer and florist business. Today it's an upscale eatery that celebrates the best of modern British cuisine with dishes like smoked eel with beetroot and fennel salad, pan-fried Cornish sole and loin of venison with spiced lentils. There's also an inventive dessert menu serving up eccentric puds – from banana Eton mess to deep-fried ice cream with strawberry salsa. Decorated with intricate ironwork flourishes and yellow checkerboard floor tiles, it's a fitting spot to celebrate a special occasion.

61–63 Banbury Road, OX2 6PE

gees-restaurant.co.uk

2

KING'S ARMS

Beloved university watering hole

Its position slap-bang in Oxford's historic centre might lead one to assume that the King's Arms is something of a tourist trap. Far from it; this authentic student pub has barely changed for generations (save for the disappearance of its men-only bar in the 1970s). When crowded, it's said that this boozer boasts the highest IQ per square foot in the world – although that mental capacity tends to diminish after the pints start flowing. It's handily placed for drinks before or after performances at the neighbouring Holywell Music Room, and no visit is complete without trying one of the pub's homemade gooey-centred scotch eggs.

40 Holywell Street, OX1 3SP
kingsarmsoxford.co.uk

3

PIERRE VICTOIRE

Bistro celebrating classic French cuisine

An Oxford institution since 1996, Pierre Victoire is a small, unfussy eatery that's about as close as you'll get to a real French bistro without crossing the Channel. But be warned, this is not a restaurant for calorie counting – its hearty prix-fixe menu will have you loosening your belt by several notches by the time the meal is over. Tuck into generous servings of *moules marinières*, melt-in-the-mouth duck leg in bitter sauce or sumptuously cheesy twice-baked Gruyère soufflé. Try, if you can, to save room for dessert – the impeccably silky crème caramel is particularly delectable.

9 Little Clarendon Street, OX1 2HP

pierrevictoire.co.uk

4

THE MAGDALEN ARMS

Gastropub serving excellent roasts

In 2009, husband-and-wife team Florence Fowler and Tony Abarno took over The Magdalen Arms and set about transforming the rough boozer into a smart gastropub. Today, it's one of the city's most highly lauded eateries with a Sunday roast that's hard to beat: plates come generously loaded with roast beef, stuffed pancetta or harissa chicken, with all the trimmings, of course. There's also a small deli at the front of the pub where you can pick up all manner of artisan larder items – from pasta to pickles – as well as giant hunks of the deliciously crisp homemade focaccia.

243 Iffley Road, OX4 1SJ
magdalenarms.co.uk

The Magdalen Arms

5

OLI'S THAI

Fresh take on Southeast Asian dining

It might be easier to get into Berghain than secure a table at Oli's Thai, but that shouldn't stop you from trying. Run by married couple Rufus and Ladd Thurston, this simple canteen is only open three days a week (Tuesday, Wednesday and Friday) and reservations book up months in advance. But if you do manage to snag one of the 22 coveted seats (or one of the four bar stools reserved for walk-ins), the rewards are plentiful. A sumptuous feast of Thai flavours awaits, with dishes such as succulent chicken thigh skewers with turmeric and coconut, rich confit duck panang curry and deep-fried sea bass with tamarind.

38 Magdalen Road, OX4 1RB

olisthai.com

6

ARBEQUINA

Sleek and simple tapas joint

Don't be fooled by the gilded 'Dispensing Chemist' sign above Arbequina's door; this former pharmacy is today a much-lauded Spanish tapas restaurant. The only prescription getting filled here is for doorstop-sized hunks of *tortilla de patatas*, succulent Ibérico tenderloin and crispy chickpea salads. Come in the evening and pull up a stool at the long zinc bar to watch chefs whipping up plates in the open kitchen. It's a satisfyingly succinct menu, accompanied by a particularly excellent cocktail list – order their Pistachio Martini or the classic *rebujito* for a refreshing blend of sherry, lemonade and mint.

72–74 Cowley Road, OX4 1JB
Other locations: The Covered Market (no.33)
arbequina.co.uk

7

TASTE TIBET

Zero-waste eatery serving authentic Tibetan food

In recent years, Magdalen Road in east Oxford has emerged as one of the city's key foodie hot spots – a reputation only strengthened by the presence of Taste Tibet. Starting as a market stall in 2014 and now a warm, unfussy restaurant, Taste Tibet is spearheaded by Tibetan Yeshi Jampa and his wife Julie Kleeman, whom he met while walking across the Himalayas to north India. Their travels are reflected in the menu: a mix of richly flavourful Himalayan curries and traditional momo dumplings (the beef and vegan options are a must), with inspiration also found in the ingredients and flavours of north India. If you're finding it tricky to settle on a dish, order the 'feast for one', which comes with two curries, rice, dal and a momo.

109 Magdalen Road, OX4 1RQ
tastetibet.com

8

GREEN ROUTES

Plant-based cafe with exceptional pancakes

Green Routes is a strong contender for the title of Oxford's best brunch destination. This cafe is run by local roastery Routes Coffee and serves the kind of plant-based food that's so tasty it attracts even the most steadfast carnivores. Its fluffy, American-style pancakes – served in an ever-changing array of sweet and savoury flavour combinations – are the real star of the show. These range from spiced apple pancakes with whipped brown sugar and smoked almond brittle (all generously doused in maple syrup) to Korean-style gochujang pancakes served with sticky 'chicken'.

39 Magdalen Road, OX4 1RB
routescoffee.co.uk/flagship

9

GEORGE & DAVIS

Homemade ice cream and decadent desserts

Back in 1992, Oxford student George Stroup opened ice cream parlour George & Davis in Jericho. The intervening decades have seen G&D's become a real community institution, with two more branches popping up in central Oxford (George & Danver) and Cowley (George & Delila). The ice cream flavours change daily but classics include Daim Bar Crunch, Oxford Blue (blueberry) and Chocolate Orange, all of which are still made on-site. If nothing tickles your fancy, you can petition for a new flavour – there's a book in each cafe where you can sign your name to lobby for new (and unusual) options. And if ice cream isn't your thing, there's plenty else on offer: from generously loaded waffles and chocolate lava cakes to freshly baked artisan bagels.

55 Little Clarendon Street, OX1 2HS
Other locations: St Aldate's, Cowley Road
gdcafe.com

10

THE PUNTER

Cosy gastropub overlooking the river

Osney Island, encircled by the Isis and a network of smaller streams, is a small residential neighbourhood made up of Victorian terraces originally built to accommodate railway workers. The building dates back to 1871, when the pub first opened as The Waterman. Today, it remains at the heart of the local community and also draws in visitors from far and wide with its excellent food. Stand-out dishes include beer-battered fish and chips and the blue cheese and squash gnocchi, which makes for excellent winter comfort food. On warmer days, there's also a quaint garden at the back where you can sit and soak up the sun with a cold glass of locally brewed ale.

7 South Street, OX2 OBE

thepunteroxford.co.uk

11

GATINEAU

Summertown's standout French patisserie

Perhaps the best reason to visit Summertown, a leafy residential neighbourhood just north of the centre, is Gatineau. This is a patisserie par excellence with irresistibly buttery croissants, crisp baguettes and melt-in-the-mouth macarons. As expected, there's a real French master baker running the show – Hervé Gatineau worked as Head of Pastry at London's Maison Blanc before opening his own namesake patisserie in 2007. His team begins work in the early hours of the morning to produce fresh pastries each day, mainly using ingredients imported from France to ensure ultimate authenticity. Arrive early to pick up a *pain aux raisins* warm from the oven and enjoy it on the sunny terrace with a *café allongé*.

209 Banbury Road, OX2 7HQ

gatineau.uk.com

12

HAMBLIN BREAD

Top-quality baked goods

Serious sourdough connoisseurs will not be disappointed by Hamblin Bread. The bakery makes its bread using stone-ground British flour, fermented slowly to produce exquisitely crusty loaves with a tender, open crumb. The original location on Iffley Road opened in 2018 and has now been joined by a second outpost in The Covered Market (no.33). It's the perfect place for a quick pick-me-up while exploring the city centre, serving takeaway coffee alongside an array of cakes and cookies. But the real pièce de résistance is their seasonal *semla* bun, a traditional Swedish confection featuring soft cardamom dough stuffed with almonds and overflowing with whipped cream.

247 Iffley Road, OX4 1SJ

Other locations: The Covered Market (no.33)

hamblinbread.co.uk

13

PROOF SOCIAL BAKEHOUSE

Bakery serving up pastries with principles

Proof Social Bakehouse offers a rare opportunity for guilt-free indulgence. Part of social enterprise Tap Social Movement (no.26), this bakery provides training and employment opportunities for prison leavers. But even without these commendable credentials, it produces the kinds of confections that are worth the 25-minute cycle from central Oxford. Located on an industrial estate at the city's southern fringe, its airy open-plan cafe is the ideal place to watch bakers shaping sourdough loaves while you sample a cardamom and blackcurrant bun or pistachio and white chocolate doughnut.

68 Sandford Lane Industrial Estate, OX1 5RP
proofbakehouse.com

SOURDOUGH £4.75

14

MISSING BEAN

Lively cafe with excellent pastries

Since opening their first coffee shop in 2009, Missing Bean founders Vicky Troth and Ori Halup have grown the business into a mini empire – with numerous locations in and around Oxford. But this original cafe is still the best. Sandwiched between colleges on picturesque Turl Street, it's constantly buzzing with students fuelling up for long library sessions. Missing Bean is more than just a stop for a quick caffeine fix, though: its counter is laden with cakes and pastries that are well worth sampling. Highlights include apple and parsnip cake topped with burnt-butter maple frosting and zingy lemon Danish pastries.

14 Turl Street, OX1 3DQ

Other locations: multiple, see website

themissingbean.co.uk

Missing Bean
coffee roasters

15

BREW

Refined Scandi-style coffee shop

BREW's minimalist interiors mirror its stripped-back approach to caffeine consumption. The menu comprises a tight selection of expertly made coffees and artisanal teas, alongside a handful of seasonal specials. Take home a bag of beans from small-batch UK roasteries or peruse the array of coffee-making accessories for yourself or the caffeine addict in your life, including sleek Japanese flasks and Hario pour-over kettles. And in case you're wondering why they sell a range of Aerobie flying rings, it's a nod to inventor Alan Adler, who also created the portable AeroPress coffee maker – in stock too, of course.

75 Banbury Road, OX2 6PE
instagram.com/brewoxford

COFFEE SHOP
BREW Est. 2013
OPEN

16

BROCHE COFFEE

Dinky coffee spot in Jericho

Oxford's 'smallest coffee shop' is – quite literally – a hole-in-the-wall setup at the end of a red-brick terrace in the heart of Jericho. And while Broche doesn't have any indoor seating, there's a small bench outside where you can sit and sip your flat white in the sun. Owner Shamsudi Tatarkhanov, who launched the cafe in 2023, also operates a small bakery unit producing fresh pastries that are lined up temptingly along Broche's window hatch. Particularly worth sampling is the *bostock* – a chunky slice of brioche that's been soaked in syrup, topped with frangipane and sprinkled with flaked almonds.

165 Kingston Road, OX2 6EG
Other locations: London Road
instagram.com/brochecoffee

BROCHE

17

BAREFOOT

Indulgent cakes for the seriously sweet-toothed

The Bruce Bogtrotter cake tells you everything you need to know about Barefoot. Named after Matilda's gluttonous schoolmate from the Roald Dahl book, this three-tiered chocolate fudge cake is the epitome of sugary decadence – generously slathered in rich buttercream and topped with hunks of salted caramel brownie. You can pick up a mammoth slice at any of the bakery's three Oxford locations, the prettiest and smallest of which is its North Parade cafe. Outwardly more beach hut than bakery, it's a cosy locale to revel in a tempting array of buns, brownies and cupcakes.

9 North Parade Avenue, OX2 6LX
Other locations: Dawson Street, Walton Street
barefootoxford.co.uk

18

LAMB & FLAG

Snug pub with literary connections

With its creaking floorboards, wood-panelled walls and Elvish script painted above the doorway, the Lamb & Flag feels every bit the Oxford literary pub of popular imagination. With roots stretching back to 1566, it became a later haunt of the Inklings – the writers' circle that included J. R. R. Tolkien and C. S. Lewis – and Thomas Hardy is said to have written parts of *Jude the Obscure* here. Today, it's run by a community-backed collective and remains wonderfully bookish: in addition to hosting book launches, on Sunday mornings, writers gather over free coffee and slices of cake to work quietly beneath its low timber beams.

12 St Giles', OX1 3JS

instagram.com/lambflagoxford

LAMB & FLAG
LAMB & FLAG
LAMB AND FLAG
FREE HOUSE
OPEN
Monday to Saturday
Sunday
Lunch served
ADT

19

EDAMAMÉ

Traditional Japanese home cooking

You'll spy this shoebox-sized eatery by the queue that forms outside its door every lunchtime. Opened in 1998 by married couple Peter and Mieko Galpin, the restaurant brings authentic Japanese dining to central Oxford. There are no reservations here; diners perch on stools around long communal tables to slurp down steaming bowls of umami-packed ramen and sticky chicken *yakisoba*. It's open in the evenings three nights a week – Thursday's sushi night is particularly popular, with ever-changing specials like scallop nigiri and beef temaki. Be sure to get there early before they start to sell out.

15 Holywell Street, OX1 3SA

edamame.co.uk

edamamé
japanese home cooking
NO BICYCLE PARKING
"the best rice and noodle dishes in town"
Lonely Planet Guide
えだまめ
営業中
OPen

20

BRANCA

Jericho's all-day eatery with a bar and deli

Spread across adjoining premises in the heart of cosmopolitan Jericho, Branca is a business in two halves. On one side is the cafe and deli that comes alive at lunchtime when its counters are filled with a buffet-style array of fresh salads and hot dishes (all doled out in generous servings). On the other side is a sleek bar and brasserie serving a seasonally changing, Mediterranean-inspired menu. On warm summer evenings, its verdant walled garden is lovely for an early evening aperitivo. And don't leave without trying their perfectly crisp and spongy focaccia, which has been freshly made daily since Branca opened in 2000.

111 Walton Street, OX2 6AJ

branca.co.uk

BRANCA
BRANCA
BRANCA

21

THE BEAR INN

Tiny boozer covered in ties

The title of 'oldest pub in Oxford' is a hotly contested one. The Bear Inn certainly has a strong claim: an inn of that name was recorded nearby as early as the 13th century. Today, it boasts everything you'd want from a homely watering hole on a chilly winter's evening: dark panelling, creaky floor, low ceilings and an open fire. What the pub is best known for, though, is the thousands of ties mounted across its walls (and ceiling). Back in the 1950s, the pub's landlord began a tradition of clipping patrons' neckties in exchange for a drink. Unfortunately, neckwear is no longer legal tender, but visit to try out the strong selection of beers on offer.

6 Alfred Street, OX1 4EH

bearoxford.co.uk

A Wide Range Of
TRADITIONAL ALES
THE BEAR
FOOD
THE BEAR
Fine Real Ales
BEER GARDEN
ALFRED ST

22

THE PERCH

Quaint pub in a tranquil setting

Situated in the tiny hamlet of Binsey, just over a mile from the city centre, The Perch feels like a step into rural Oxfordshire. The thatched roof and crackling open fire in winter only add to its storybook charm. The food is excellent (don't leave without ordering one of their famous pies) but the real draw is the setting. Overlooked by willow trees, the pub's leafy garden is separated from the sprawling greenery of Port Meadow (no.53) by the meandering River Thames, known locally as the Isis. Arrive on foot for the full experience: a short hike across the meadow, via a wooden bridge, delivers you to a picturesque riverside path snaking all the way to the pub.

Binsey Lane, OX2 0NG

the-perch.co.uk

23

TURF TAVERN

Hidden watering hole with ancient roots

Concealed in the shadow of the old city wall, Turf Tavern is linked to nearby streets by a tangle of narrow alleyways. Despite its secluded location, assume that anyone who's anyone has visited, including Elizabeth Taylor, David Bowie and Ernest Hemingway. It also lays claim to being the site where future Australian prime minister Bob Hawke set a Guinness World Record for downing a yard of ale in 11 seconds, and where Bill Clinton famously smoked marijuana but 'didn't inhale'. And while the food may not be the pub's strong point, its courtyard – hemmed in by ivy-clad medieval walls – is one of the city's most scenic settings for a pint on a sunny day.

4 Bath Place, OX1 3SU

greeneking.co.uk/pubs/oxfordshire/turf-tavern

BATH PLACE
Oxford
17th
Century
Hotel
Tel: 01865
791812
The Famous
Turf Tavern
A VERY WARM
Welcome
AWAITS....
AN EDUCATION
IN INTOXICATION

24

BROWN'S CAFE

Classic caff serving hearty breakfasts

This old-school greasy spoon might not be the city's swankiest eatery, but what it lacks in culinary finesse it makes up for in retro appeal. It's a favourite among students looking to revive themselves after a heavy night on the town. Here in a corner of The Covered Market (no.33), you'll find peaky-looking undergraduates fixing their hangovers with bacon butties and large mugs of milky tea. Brown's has been an Oxford institution since 1920, beloved for its no-frills charm and generous full English breakfasts (complete with artery-clogging fried bread). And don't worry if you don't manage to get there in the morning; fry-ups are served all day.

The Covered Market, Market Street, OX1 3DY
oxford-coveredmarket.co.uk/traders/browns

Brown's
CAFÉ
Brown's
CAFÉ
Est. 1924
Brown's
CAFÉ
Est. 1924

25

THE CHESTER ARMS

Cheery pub with a famous steak platter

The Chester Arms is a friendly neighbourhood pub in the heart of Iffley Fields, a patch of Victorian terraces in east Oxford that gives way to the meadows running along the Isis. The pub is renowned for its signature dish: a hearty pile of sliced beef onglet served with chunky chips, béarnaise sauce, cabbage with bacon and fresh salad. These plentiful platters are available only for two or three to share, but luckily for solo diners there's plenty else on the menu (the chicken burger with homemade BBQ sauce is particularly tasty). And be sure to look out for the dog wall, which is covered with Polaroid portraits of the pub's beloved canine visitors.

19 Chester Street, OX4 1SN
chesterarmsoxford.co.uk

26

TAP SOCIAL MOVEMENT

Brewery and events space with social purpose

An industrial estate in Botley might seem an unlikely setting for one of Oxford's best watering holes. Tap Social Movement, however, has built a fiercely loyal following at its warehouse taproom. Founded in 2017, this independent brewery and social enterprise combines excellent craft beer with an ambitious rehabilitation programme, providing training and employment for people leaving prison. In summer, long communal tables spill out across the yard, where locals gather over hoppy pale ales, Belgian-inspired sours and seasonal brews infused with local fruits and herbs. There's a lively calendar of events, too, ranging from live music and yoga classes to wrestling matches and community fundraisers.

Curtis Industrial Estate, North Hinksey Lane, OX2 0LX

tapsocialmovement.com

27
CHERWELL BOATHOUSE

Family-run riverside eatery and punting station

A fixture of Oxford life for more than half a century, this smart restaurant remains a favourite among residents of the city's affluent northern suburbs. Located at the end of a leafy lane, it sits beside the Cherwell, with tables just metres from the water. Set within an Edwardian boathouse – which still operates as a punting station – the restaurant offers idyllic views of the willow tree-lined riverbanks and rolling meadows beyond. The menu has been carefully constructed by head chef Paul Bell to put an international spin on modern British cuisine, featuring dishes such as Cotswold chicken breast with spiced tomato salsa and monkfish with a tarragon velouté.

50 Bardwell Road, OX2 6ST
cherwellboathouse.co.uk

Push bar to open
Push bar to open

28

SCRIPTUM

Pen and paper paradise

A shrine to the written word, Scriptum is Oxford's premier spot for stationery. It's a neat encapsulation of the city's eccentric, old-world charm – with sumptuous window displays and snug interiors decorated with marble busts, Persian rugs and antique dark wood furniture. From feather quills to fountain pens, every imaginable writing implement can be found here, alongside a range of old-school desk staples, including paperweights, inkwells and wax seals. Naturally, there are all manner of notebooks; splash out by having an Italian leather-bound journal engraved with your initials in gold or silver for an additional fee.

3 Turl Street, OX1 3DQ
scriptum.co.uk

29

OBJECTS OF USE

The traditional hardware shop reimagined

Ever wondered where you could pick up a goat-hair brush designed specifically for cleaning Venetian blinds? How about an Indonesian carpet beater, or compostable loofah? Objects of Use is home to everything you never knew you needed. This pocket-sized emporium enjoys a cult following among design aficionados who are drawn to owner Hazel Rattigan's carefully curated selection of top-quality basics that stylishly combine form and function. Stock is sourced from small producers around the world, with items all laid out across shelves and tables in irresistibly neat formations – making it a hardware shop unlike any other.

6 Lincoln House, Market Street, OX1 3EQ

objectsofuse.com

MARIUS FABRE
KNOX

Objects of Use
Objects of Use

Objects of Use
Objects of Use

30

JERICHO CHEESE COMPANY

Premium cheesemonger and deli

From Caerphilly to Wensleydale, this den of dairy delights stocks the finest cheeses from across Britain and Ireland. Cheesemonger Adam Verlander set up his first store on Little Clarendon Street in 2016, with the help of his former employer, the acclaimed Neal's Yard Dairy. A second shop followed a few years later in central Oxford. Both have stylishly pared-back interiors and counters stacked with huge hunks of Cheddar, Stilton and Red Leicester. And if you must pick just one, the Rollright from Gloucestershire's King Stone Dairy – a soft, creamy cheese with a distinctive smoky aroma – is particularly irresistible.

25 Little Clarendon Street, OX1 2HU
Other locations: Ship Street
jerichocheese.co.uk

JERICHO CHEESE COMPANY
JERICHO CHEESE COMPANY

31

2 NORTH PARADE

Farmers' market condensed into pint-sized deli

Opened in 2013, 2 North Parade stocks seasonal produce from organic farms around Oxford, all arranged in wooden crates, wicker baskets and enamel bowls on counters like an old-school greengrocer. In spring, there are even bundles of fresh asparagus delivered daily by bicycle from nearby Medley Manor Farm. You'll also find a selection of British farmhouse cheeses, hand-made jams and locally cured meats. Look out for pastries from micro-bakery Pet Gât, stocking the deli with some exceptionally delicious confections, from almond and saffron buns to blueberry and lavender tartlets.

2 North Parade Avenue, OX2 6LX

instagram.com/2northparade

Secateurs
Secateurs
Secateurs

32

GULP FICTION

Bookshop, cafe and bar, all under one historic roof

Gulp Fiction is more than just a place to pick up a new novel; this bookshop in The Covered Market (no.33) doubles as a cafe during the week. Browse the books bearing a sticker that promises a free coffee with purchase, then settle into the comfy, lounge-like space upstairs and bury your head in the pages. For a livelier experience, head to Gulp Fiction on a Thursday, Friday or Saturday evening, when it transforms into a buzzy bar with a varied programme of in-store events, hosting everything from book launches and author talks to literary quizzes and live jazz performances.

The Covered Market, Market Street, OX1 3DU
gulpfictionbooks.com

(A-Z by Author)
Fiction
Fiction
Ian McEwan
What We Can Know
ZADIE SMITH SWING TIME
David Szalay
FLESH
CIRCE
TOP SHELF FICTION
Hardback Classics
MAGGIE FARRELL
THE MARRIAGE PORTRAIT
DONNA TARTT
THE MIDNIGHT LIBRARY
MATT HAIG
NORMAL PEOPLE
SALLY ROONEY
Orbital

33

THE COVERED MARKET

Centuries-old shopping arcade

Just behind Cornmarket Street – once Oxford's main shopping street, now an underwhelming mix of chains and tourist-tat stores – is a thriving hub of independent businesses. The Covered Market (as you might guess from the name) brings together all manner of shops and cafes under one roof. Established more than 250 years ago, it was purpose-built to clear the city streets of obstructive market stalls, later surviving proposals for demolition and relocation. Today, within its wooden arcades you'll find everything from upscale watch sellers and florists to pie shops and pizzerias.

Market Street, OX1 3DZ
oxford-coveredmarket.co.uk

GEORGINAS
Coffee shop
THE
CAKE
SHOP
GEORGINAS
Coffee shop

34

BLACKWELL'S

Oxford's biggest bookshop

Considering Oxford (supposedly) boasts more published authors per square mile than any other city in Europe, it's no surprise that it's also home to one of the world's largest bookshops. Blackwell's small storefront belies its Tardis-like interior: the shop spreads across four floors, the largest of which is the cavernous basement filled with three miles of bookshelves. And while Blackwell's specialises in academic texts (with a generous discount for Oxford students and alumni), you'll find every imaginable kind of book here, from antiquarian volumes of Italian poetry to modern romance novels. Sound overwhelming? Friendly staff are on hand to recommend new titles using their encyclopaedic literary knowledge.

48–51 Broad Street, OX1 3BQ
blackwells.co.uk

51 BLACKWELL 50

35

GOODIES

Stylish menswear store showcasing British craft

Oxford might have its fair share of high street clothing shops, but when it comes to modern apparel from smaller labels, Goodies stands out. Adding a touch of contemporary cool to the storied atmosphere of The Covered Market (no.33), this small, whitewashed shop carries a refined selection of quality menswear. From traditional fisherman's jumpers knitted in Guernsey to cotton jackets handsewn in Great Yarmouth, most of their stock is made in Britain – keep an eye out for their range of neatly tailored Japanese denim, though. And if you're dithering over the perfect fit, owner Matt Evans, a stylist who opened the shop with his wife Rachael in 2024, is on hand to advise.

The Covered Market, Market Street, OX1 3DX

instagram.com/goodiesoxford

GOODIES

DO ONE THING WELL
IT'S ENOUGH.
FEELING GOOD

TENDER
COMPLETE

36

TRUCK

Oxford's premier record shop

Given that it's synonymous with high-minded scholarliness, it might surprise you that Oxford is home to a thriving alternative music scene. This is the city, after all, that gave us Radiohead. At the centre of it all is Truck, a beloved record shop that opened in 2011 as an offshoot of the Truck Festival. Its shelves are packed with new releases, classic albums and pre-loved finds on both vinyl and CD, alongside indie-exclusive pressings and specialist genre titles. The shop also hosts album launches and intimate in-store performances, while a small counter serving drinks from Mostro Coffee makes lingering between the racks all the more tempting.

101 Cowley Road, OX4 1HU

truckmusic.store

UK
2025
kins
DEYA
STUDIO
WAR child
#RSD25
NEW
LIN
M
THE LINDA

37

DAUNT BOOKS

Inviting bookshop with old-school charm

While Daunt Books might be part of a chain (albeit an independent one), it boasts all the cosy appeal of a neighbourhood bookshop – the kind it's hard to leave without a hardback in hand. Today it's something of a cornerstone for Summertown's bookish local community (which includes a high density of university professors) who flock to its regular in-store author talks. Particularly worth perusing are the offerings from Daunt's in-house publishing arm, from exciting debut writers to beautiful new editions of rediscovered classics. And be sure to take your purchases home in a Daunt Books tote bag – the ultimate signifier of literary superiority.

247–249 Banbury Road, OX2 7HN
summertown.dauntbooks.co.uk

BOOKS
249
DAUNT
BOOKS

38

HOYLE'S OF OXFORD

Eclectic games emporium

No matter how you feel about organised fun, it's hard not to be charmed by Hoyle's. This small, family-run shop crams far more than Monopoly and chess sets into its shelves: walls are stacked high with everything from 100-sided dice to vampire-themed role-playing games. Head to the back of the store and you'll find a trove of vintage curiosities, including 1930s bagatelle boards and domino sets dating back to the 1800s. The shop takes its name from the 18th-century writer Edmond Hoyle, whose name lives on in the legendary *Hoyle's Rules of Games* – a copy of which you can pick up here too, of course.

71 High Street, OX1 4BA
hoylesoxford.com

HOYLE'S OF OXFORD
HOYLE'S OF OXFORD
HOYLE'S OF OXFORD
HOYLE'S
CHESS & BACKGAMMON
PUZZLES · PLAYING CARDS
BOARD GAMES · JIGSAWS
71

39

BODLEIAN LIBRARY

Veritable bibliophile's sanctuary

The Bodleian – Oxford University's principal library – is Britain's second-largest library, with over 14 million printed items held at its various sites. The original library, opened in 1602, centres around an elaborately carved stone courtyard, which you can freely wander around. As its collections grew over the centuries, the library expanded into neighbouring buildings, including the circular Radcliffe Camera, arguably Oxford's most iconic landmark. It's well worth doing a guided tour to really take in the key sights, such as the medieval Duke Humfrey's Library (where scenes from the first Harry Potter film were shot) and the Divinity School, Oxford's oldest teaching room and a marvel of Gothic architecture.

Broad Street, OX1 3BG

bodleian.ox.ac.uk

STEES COLL: OMN: ANIM: ÆD: XTI: CYRILLVS COBB DONALDVS HYDE

ALII TAM AMERICANI QVAM BRITANNICI. HINC SCIAS AMICVS FIDELIS PROTECTIO
25

40

PITT RIVERS MUSEUM

Eccentric cabinet of curiosities

Lovers of the weird and wonderful will be charmed by this eccentric repository. Founded in 1884 after General Augustus Pitt Rivers donated his vast personal collection to the University of Oxford, the museum today holds more than 500,000 objects, photographs and manuscripts from across the globe. Unusually, its displays are organised not by geography or chronology but by object type – such as masks, instruments and weapons – creating what curators describe as a 'democracy of things'. The effect is gloriously random; weave between crowded glass cases packed with finds from every corner of human history, including Hawaiian ceremonial capes and Siberian reindeer-skin underwear.

South Parks Road, OX1 3PP

prm.ox.ac.uk

41

THE ULTIMATE PICTURE PALACE

Charming community-owned cinema in Cowley

Opened in 1911, The Ultimate Picture Palace is Oxford's oldest independent cinema – and it proudly wears its age on its sleeve. Tucked away off Cowley Road, this single-screen picture house has long been a refuge for film buffs, students and couples seeking a more characterful date locale than a multiplex. Original features like the vintage ticket booth and red velvet curtains remain intact, while the programme ranges from Hollywood classics and cult favourites to foreign-language films and local festival screenings. There's also a licensed bar – within the auditorium itself – serving wine, beer and ice cream, courtesy of local makers G&D's (no.9).

Jeune Street, OX4 1BN

uppcinema.com

THE ULTIMATE PICTURE PALACE
DAHOMEY
FIGHT NIGHTS

42

ASHMOLEAN MUSEUM

Treasure trove of art and artefacts

Oxford is a historian's playground – and there's nowhere better to marvel at wonders from across the ages than Britain's first public museum. Founded in 1683, it houses the university's collection of art and archaeology – rather like the British Museum and National Gallery rolled into one. Here, you'll find everything from Japanese samurai armour to Guy Fawkes' lantern alongside paintings from the likes of Manet, Turner and Picasso. You could easily spend a whole day exploring its hallowed halls, but if you're pressed for time, make a beeline for the Ancient World galleries to discover Egyptian mummies, Assyrian reliefs and Roman sculpture.

Beaumont Street, OX1 2PH

ashmolean.org

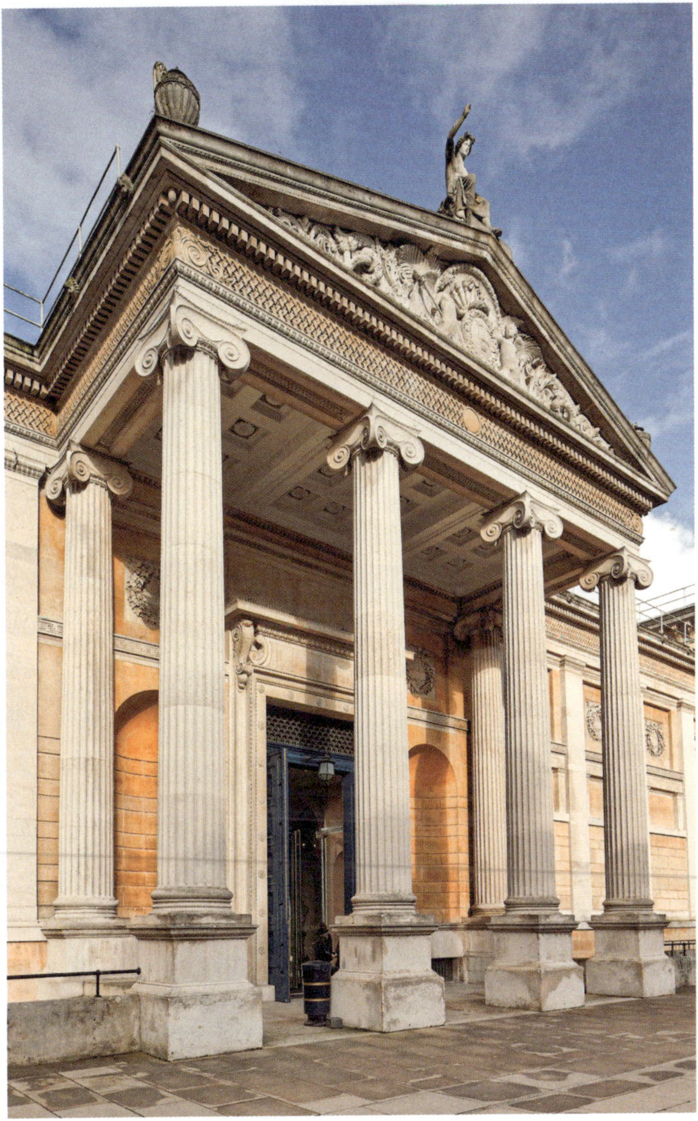

DYNASTIC E D NUBIA
HE CHRISTIAN

43

OXFORD PLAYHOUSE

Art Deco design and impressive patrons

Founded in 1928, the Oxford Playhouse has hosted generations of British acting talent to its stage. In its early years, a resident company of actors would perform one production in the evenings while rehearsing the next by day – a relentless theatrical rhythm that helped shape the careers of countless performers. Today, its patrons include Dame Judi Dench (who was a member of the repertory company in the 1960s), as well as Michael Palin and Rowan Atkinson, both of whom performed here while students at the university. With its Georgian-style facade and handsome Art Deco interiors, the venue remains one of Oxford's cultural anchors, with a diverse programme of touring West End productions, experimental drama, comedy, dance and family shows.

11–12 Beaumont Street, OX1 2LW

oxfordplayhouse.com

PLAYHOUSE
Breaking the Code
The Talented Mr. Ripley

44

OXFORD UNIVERSITY MUSEUM OF NATURAL HISTORY

Victorian museum celebrating the natural world

Few buildings in Oxford inspire childlike wonder quite like this spectacular museum. Opened in 1860, it's housed inside a dramatic neo-Gothic building with a soaring glass roof. Cloistered arcades wrap around the vast central court, their columns built using different varieties of British stone and decorated with intricate patterns of leaves and flowers. On display is everything from towering dinosaur skeletons to glittering mineral displays, as well as all manner of taxidermy birds and animals. Lewis Carroll would often wander the hall in search of inspiration for his fantastical worlds, famously basing his dodo character in *Alice*'s *Adventures in Wonderland* on the museum's reconstruction of the bird.

Parks Road, OX1 3PW

oumnh.ox.ac.uk

POSITIVE ACTION

45

MODERN ART OXFORD

Contemporary art gallery with big-name exhibitors

While most visit Oxford for the city's historic charm, it can be refreshing to balance the ancient with the contemporary by dropping in to Modern Art Oxford. Nestled on a side street near the Westgate shopping centre, the gallery is among the UK's preeminent contemporary art spaces. Founded by architect Trevor Green in 1965, it moved to this former brewery site a year later and has since exhibited works by leading global artists, including the likes of Yoko Ono, Carl Andre and Tracey Emin. Don't forget to check out the cafe while you're there and take in the colourful interiors designed by artist Emma Hart.

30 Pembroke Street, OX1 1BP

modernartoxford.org.uk

Modern Art Oxford

Modern Art Oxford
PENCIL SET
Modern Art Oxford
HIPHIP
HOORAY

Modern Art Oxford
Modern Art Oxford

46

OLD FIRE STATION

Performing arts venue and charity hub

Old Fire Station is a nexus of community and creativity, driven by social purpose. By day, it's a place where people experiencing homelessness can access vital training and support from charity Crisis. By night, it's a buzzy locale for live music, theatre and dance that also regularly hosts some of the UK's top stand-up comedy acts. In recent years, Old Fire Station has also become known as one of the city's best-loved eateries, thanks to the work of Damascus Rose Kitchen, a social enterprise that takes over the cafe from Tuesday to Saturday, serving authentic Middle Eastern dishes prepared by refugee women.

40 George Street, OX1 2AQ
oldfirestation.org.uk

Crisis
What's On

47

CHRIST CHURCH

Literary and architectural crowd-puller

For many visitors, Christ Church is the first stop on the Oxford checklist. Architecturally speaking, it's astounding: the main quadrangle is the city's largest, with a medieval cathedral at its heart and a Sir Christopher Wren-designed tower over the gate. Its Great Hall inspired Hogwarts in the Harry Potter films, helping explain the near-constant crowds. But that's not the only literary connection. Lewis Carroll studied and taught here, befriending the Dean's daughter, Alice, who inspired the protagonist in his fantastical novels. The two would often go on picnics in the adjoining Christ Church Meadow, where visitors can amble along riverside paths and admire postcard views of Oxford's famous spires.

St Aldate's, OX1 1DP

chch.ox.ac.uk

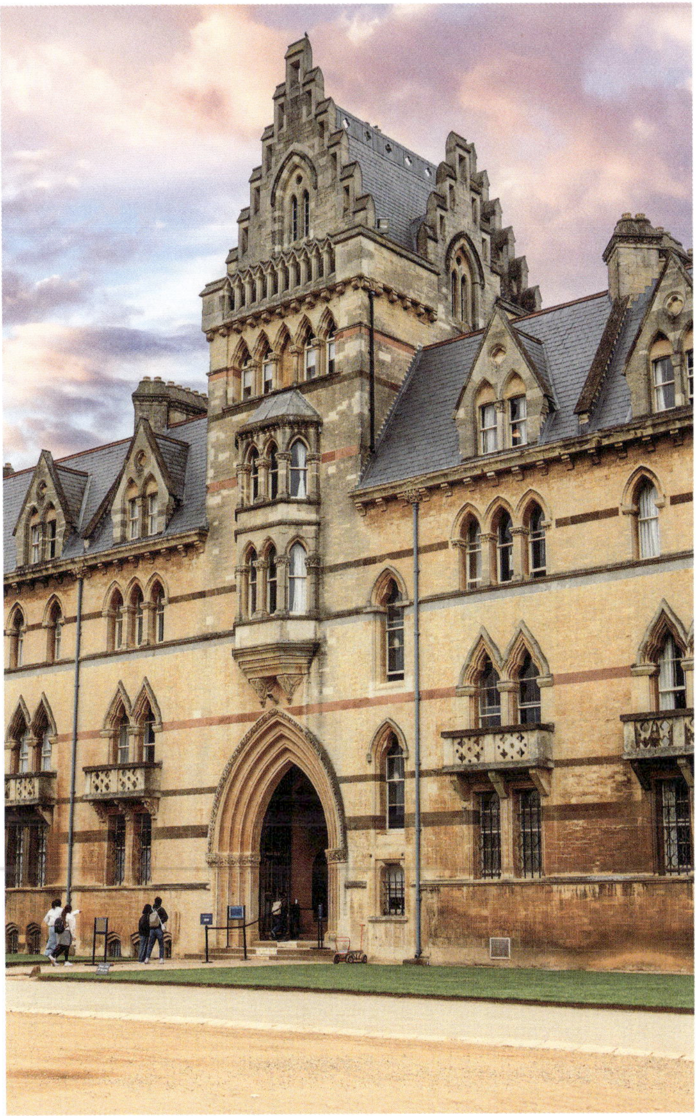

48

NEW COLLEGE

Visitor-friendly college with a picturesque garden

Only by Oxford standards could this college be considered 'new'. Founded in 1379, New College set the architectural standard for all future colleges with its front quadrangle design, consisting of a chapel, library, dining hall and a home for the Warden (the head of the college) above the gate tower. From March to October, it admits visitors seven days a week to its grand, wood-panelled dining hall and ornately decorated chapel, which features surviving medieval stained glass. Its gardens are also some of the finest in Oxford, with one of the country's longest herbaceous borders and an imposing ornamental mound (which looks a bit like a Mayan temple) at its centre.

Holywell Street, OX1 3BN

new.ox.ac.uk

CONDIS DEXTRA. CONDIS COLLEGIA
TUARUM UNAM VICIT UTRAQUE

49

MAGDALEN COLLEGE

Get lost in the grounds of this hallowed institution

Given that Magdalen is renowned as one of Oxford's most beautiful colleges, it's particularly convenient that it's also one of the easiest to visit. Locals can visit free of charge; otherwise, a £10 ticket will let you have a poke around the chapel (complete with impossibly intricate carved stonework), the dark wood-panelled dining hall and 15th-century cloisters. But what really sets Magdalen apart is its lush, manicured gardens and 100 acres of grounds. Snaking around its iconic Water Meadow is a scenic footpath known as Addison's Walk, a favourite of C. S. Lewis's when he was a Fellow and Tutor at the college. As you explore, keep an eye out for kingfishers, otters and herons, as well as Magdalen's own herd of fallow deer.

High Street, OX1 4AU

magd.ox.ac.uk

50

MAGDALEN BRIDGE

Riverside spot for punting

Punting is *the* quintessential Oxford summer pastime. Like a Venetian gondolier, you propel the boat along – though rather less glamorously, by pushing a long pole against the riverbed instead of using an oar. But don't be fooled by practised boatmen gliding effortlessly along; getting to grips with punting takes time, so hiring a punt 'chauffeur' for an hour may be money well spent. Magdalen Bridge punting station is a convenient city-centre base for hiring boats – from here, the standard route heads downstream past Christ Church Meadow. That said, upstream is a quieter (and perhaps prettier) option, with gardens, parks and meadows on either bank.

Magdalen Bridge, OX1 4AU
oxfordpunting.co.uk

51

BLENHEIM PALACE

Grand Baroque palace and birthplace of Churchill

When the first Duke of Marlborough trounced the French at the Battle of Blenheim in 1704, the nation dug deep into its pockets to show its gratitude. The result was Blenheim Palace, a massive Baroque residence set in 2,000 acres of landscaped parkland, still home today to the duke's descendants. It's a UNESCO World Heritage Site with huge tourist pulling power, so get there early to avoid the crowds. Buses run regularly from the city centre, less than ten miles away, arriving at the palace's gates near the pretty market town of Woodstock (well worth a stroll when you've finished up at the palace).

Woodstock, OX20 1UL

blenheimpalace.com

52

OXFORD BOTANIC GARDEN

Plant-lover's paradise

Set on the site of the city's medieval Jewish cemetery, the Oxford Botanic Garden was founded in 1621, making it the oldest of its kind in Britain. An oasis of diversity (part scientific institution, part botanical wonder), it's still owned by the university and used for growing research specimens. Within its pleasant walled gardens, you'll find some 5,000 species, from a giant waterlily (whose robust leaves can carry the weight of a small child) to carnivorous butterworts and bladderworts. In summer, it's the perfect picnic site (no booze allowed, though) and in the winter months, its large glasshouses provide a tropical escape from the drizzle.

Rose Lane, OX1 4AZ
obga.ox.ac.uk/visit-garden

53

PORT MEADOW

Sweeping riverside grassland

Central Oxford is surrounded by floodplains that can't be developed, meaning the countryside flows right into the town. The largest and most idyllic stretch is Port Meadow, a huge swathe of 300 acres that transforms with the seasons. Spring showers see the meadow submerged under water, dry summers make its grasses ideal for sunbathing, while winter frosts cause the vast pool at its centre to freeze – look out for locals whizzing around on ice skates. But it's at its most hauntingly beautiful on autumn evenings as the sun sets and ground mist begins to form, the swooping silhouettes of honking geese overhead.

Walton Well Road, OX2 6ED

oxford.gov.uk/directory-record/673/port-meadow

MAD MARCH
HARE
BOAT
COMPANY
No 14

54

UNIVERSITY PARKS

Sprawling lawns for sports and strolling

Within walking distance of the city centre, these 74 acres of greenery offer both a restful escape and a sports ground for the university. Pitches host everything – from cricket and football to croquet and even, yes, Quidditch – but luckily the park's size means these sporting activities don't spoil the peace. It's a favourite among dog walkers from the well-heeled north Oxford suburbs as well as picnickers who lay down their rugs along the riverbank. The park is also home to a remarkable assortment of trees from around the globe, its avenues fringed with towering specimens including Japanese pagoda trees and soaring Californian sequoias.

South Parks Road, OX1 3RF

parks.ox.ac.uk

55

OXFORD CANAL

Leafy waterside walk providing peace and quiet

Oxford might not be the world's most frenetic metropolis, but when the tourist crowds descend over summer months, a stroll along the canal can offer a welcome change of pace. Constructed to carry coal into the city, today it's all tree-lined tranquillity – a slow, winding towpath stretching from the city centre into open countryside. You'll pass narrowboats, an abundance of birdlife, as well as handsome Victorian houses with gardens trailing down to the water. If you're looking for an extended walk, continue along the path for some three miles to reach the small village of Wolvercote, where you can wet your whistle at country pub The Plough.

canalrivertrust.org.uk/canals-and-rivers/oxford-canal

56

HARCOURT ARBORETUM

Dreamy woodland wonderland

Harcourt Arboretum feels a world away from the bustle of the city. Run by the Oxford Botanic Garden (no.52), the 130-acre site was established in 1835 and today contains some of Britain's oldest redwoods, alongside wildflower meadows, orchards and a particularly striking collection of rhododendrons and magnolias in spring. Peacocks roam freely through the grounds, often appearing with little warning from behind hedges or beneath towering conifers. It's especially lovely in autumn, when the Japanese maples turn fiery shades of crimson and orange. To get there, it's a 30-minute bus ride from the city centre. Be sure to allow plenty of time to wander the winding paths.

Oxford Lodge, Peacock Gate, OX44 9PX
obga.ox.ac.uk/visit-arboretum

57

HINKSEY OUTDOOR POOL

Cheery neighbourhood lido

On hot summer days, Oxford residents flock here armed with towels, paperbacks and supermarket meal deals. Opened in 1936, this much-loved open-air lido sits just beyond the city centre and is said to be one of the largest outdoor swimming pools in the south of England. Serious swimmers carve up lanes at one end while students and families sprawl across the lawn in the sunshine, shadowed by willow trees. There's a small cafe for post-swim coffees and ice cream, though many regulars prefer to picnic beside the water and stay until closing time.

Hinksey Park, OX1 4RP

oxfordcityleisure.com/hinksey-outdoor-pool

58

THE NETTY

Oxford's smallest (and most eccentric) hotel

Oxford is a city of oddities, but its curios don't get much more curious than this two-suite hotel. Hidden beneath the busy traffic island at St Giles', this unusual boutique stay occupies a pair of restored Victorian public toilets inherited from 1895. Thankfully, little remains of their former purpose beyond the original tiles and wrought iron details. Today, the subterranean suites are decked out with jewel-toned furnishings courtesy of interior designer Rachael Gowdridge; vintage lamps, French tapestries and plump velvet headrests make them feel more Wes Anderson than public convenience. Guests descend directly from the street – via a set of tiled steps – into cosy underground rooms lit by pavement glass overhead.

1A St Giles', OX1 3JS

thenetty.co.uk

59

OLD PARSONAGE HOTEL

Snug bolthole with storied charm

If it's cosiness you're after, look no further than the Old Parsonage Hotel. Set inside a wisteria-clad building which has stood since 1660, this hotel would not be out of place in a Cotswolds village. In winter, a roaring log fire greets visitors at reception, with the restaurant beyond luring you further in with the snug appeal of its deep plum-painted walls and the promise of a hearty lunch. Upstairs, its 35 rooms and suites are quietly luxurious with their handmade beds, thoughtfully curated selection of artworks and sleek marble bathrooms. Guests can also make use of free bicycle hire; handy, given that two wheels is the best way to explore Oxford.

1–3 Banbury Road, OX2 6NN
oldparsonagehotel.co.uk

OXFORD COLLECTION

Churchill & Son

60

OLD BANK HOTEL

Art-filled lodgings in a former bank

Just a stone's throw from the Radcliffe Camera (part of the Bodleian Library, no.39), the Old Bank Hotel is probably Oxford's most central hotel. Its spacious rooftop suite – aptly named 'The Room With The View' – offers close-up vistas of All Souls College and the ornate Gothic spire of the University Church of St Mary the Virgin. Such perks come with a hefty price tag, naturally. The hotel's 43 rooms are stylishly pared-back, decorated with a tasteful mix of contemporary artworks selected from owner Jeremy Mogford's personal collection. Even if you're not staying, its restaurant Quod is a reliably excellent spot for long lunches and celebratory dinners. And if it's sunny, try to nab a table on the inviting outdoor terrace.

92–94 High Street, OX1 4BJ
oldbankhotel.co.uk

OLD
BANK
HOTEL

61

ESTELLE MANOR

Lavish country pile loved by the glitterati

Lodgings don't get much swankier than Estelle Manor. This luxurious private members' club and hotel – set within a Grade II-listed Jacobean-style manor house – lies just outside North Leigh, a small village 20 minutes' drive from central Oxford. It sits amid 3,000 acres of rolling parkland, with rooms and suites spread across woodland cabins, individual cottages and, of course, the opulently decorated main house. A-listers flock here on mini breaks from London, enjoying lavish meals at the four on-site restaurants and unwinding at Eynsham Baths – the vast, Roman-inspired bath-house complete with a marble-clad tepidarium, caldarium and a heated outdoor pool.

Eynsham Park, OX29 6PN

estellemanor.com

ABOUT THE AUTHOR

Hester Underhill grew up in Oxford, and today works as a freelance writer focusing on culture and design. She is the founder of online film magazine *Cinemagoer* and her work has appeared in *The New York Times*, *Financial Times* and *The Guardian*. Find her on Instagram @hesteru.

ABOUT HOXTON MINI PRESS

Hoxton Mini Press is a small indie publisher based in east London. We make beautiful books with a dedication to sustainable production and great photography.

When we started the company, people told us print was dead; we wanted to prove them wrong. Books are no longer just about information, but objects to collect and own.

We promise three things. Firstly, nothing in this guidebook is sponsored; it's our own independent opinion. Secondly, our books are 100 per cent carbon compensated with printing, paper and transport fully offset. And finally, everything is researched, edited and written by humans.

IMAGE CREDITS

Page 2 © Ugur Akdemir / Unsplash; Page 4 © Alex Thomson; Page 5 © Mark Anthony Fox; Page 6 © Jon Day; Page 8 © Objects of Use; Page 9 © Alex Thomson; Gees © Carol Sachs; King's Arms first image © Cintia Rezende, second image © Matt Austin; Pierre Victoire © Phyllis Chow / @121.days; The Madgalen Arms © Patricia Niven; Oli's Thai © Paul Gregory; Arbequina © Paul Gregory; Taste Tibet © Paul Gregory; Green Routes © Matt Budd; George & Davis © George & Davis; The Punter © The Punter; Gatineau © Oliver Mohr; Hamblin Bread © Danni Maibaum; Proof Social Bakehouse © Imogen Florence; Missing Bean © Missing Bean; BREW © Alex Thomson; Broche Coffee © Luke Hayes; Barefoot © John Blackwell; Lamb & Flag © Wirestock / Dreamstime.com; Edamamé © David McGill / Alamy; Branca © David Fisher; The Bear Inn © Fuller, Smith and Turner; The Perch © The Perch; Turf Tavern © Imagebroker.com / Alamy; Brown's Cafe © Porcelain Photography / Alamy; The Chester Arms © The Chester Arms; Tap Social Movement © Will Elsom; Cherwell Boathouse first image © Jeff Gilbert / Alamy, second image © Francisco Martinez / Alamy; Scriptum © Scriptum; Objects of Use © Objects of Use; Jericho Cheese Company © Alex Thomson; 2 North Parade © 2 North Parade; Gulp Fiction © Gulp Fiction; The Covered Market © Mark Bassett / Alamy; Blackwell's © Eye Ubiquitous / Alamy; Goodies © David Fisher; Truck © Ian Hanham; Daunt Books © Elizabeth Perry; Hoyle's of Oxford © Hoyle's of Oxford; Bodleian Library © Christopher John; Pitt Rivers Museum © John Cairns, Pitt Rivers Museum, University of Oxford; The Ultimate Picture Palace © Monika Tomiczek, Oxford Atelier; Ashmolean Museum first image © Archimage / Alamy, second and third image © Ashmolean Museum; Oxford Playhouse © Andrew Walmsley; Oxford University Museum of Natural History first image © RW, second image © Sam Allard; Modern Art Oxford © Dan Weill; Old Fire Station © Old Fire Station; Christ Church first image © Adobe Stock, second image © Alfredo Garcia Saz / Adobe Stock, third image © Andrei Nekrassov / Adobe Stock; New College © Florie Harmer; Magdalen College first image © John and Tina Reid / Getty, second image © Bloomberg / Getty; Magdalen Bridge © Angus McComiskey / Alamy; Blenheim Palace © Blenheim Palace Heritage Foundation; Oxford Botanic Garden first image © Andrei Nekrassov / Alamy, second image © Chon Kit Leong / Alamy, third image © Andrew Daymond / Alamy; Port Meadow first image © Anthony P Morris, Farmoor / Alamy, second image © Kevin White / Getty; University Parks © Alex Thomson; Oxford Canal © Alex Thomson; Harcourt Arboretum © Anthony P Morris, Farmoor / Alamy; Hinksey Outdoor Pool © G.P. Essex / Alamy; The Netty © Dean Hearne; Old Parsonage Hotel first image © Carol Sachs, second image © Peter Jackson; Old Bank Hotel first image © Quintin Lake, second image © Peter Jackson; Estelle Manor © Mark Anthony Fox.

An Opinionated Guide to Oxford
First edition, first printing

Published in 2026 by Hoxton Mini Press, London.

Text by Hester Underhill
Editing by Olivia Kumar
Production design by Dom Grant
Production control by David Brimble
Proofreading by Emma Seckel
Editorial support by Kate Overy
& Emma Seckel

With thanks to Matthew Young for initial series design.

Please note: we recommend checking the websites listed for each entry before you visit for the latest information on price, opening times and pre-booking requirements.

Thank you to all of the individuals and institutions who have provided images and arranged permissions. While every effort has been made to trace the present copyright holders we apologise in advance for any unintentional omission or error, and would be pleased to insert the appropriate acknowledgement in any subsequent edition.

A CIP catalogue record for this book is available from the British Library.

ISBN: 978-1-917719-41-4

Printed and bound by OZGraf, Poland

Manufacturer: Hoxton Mini Press, 104 Northside Studios, 16–29 Andrews Road, London E8 4QF, UK
www.hoxtonminipress.com

Represented by: Authorised Rep Compliance Ltd., Ground Floor, 71 Lower Baggot Street, Dublin D02 P593, Ireland
www.arccompliance.com

Hoxton Mini Press is an environmentally conscious publisher, committed to offsetting our carbon footprint. This book is 100 per cent carbon compensated, with offset purchased from Stand For Trees.

Every time you order from our website, we plant a tree: www.hoxtonminipress.com

FSC
www.fsc.org
MIX
Paper | Supporting responsible forestry
FSC® C163799

Selected opinionated guides in the series:

For more go to www.hoxtonminipress.com

INDEX